What Others Are Saying About This Book:

"Griff has a long history of motivating business people and assisting businesses in strategic planning. That history is reflected in this book, and his approach to starting a business is universal -- these 10 Questions apply to any business.

His thoughts about the answers apply to any individual and include very direct steps in analyzing their personal characteristics and how they apply to becoming an entrepreneur."

Kent Smith
Senior Corporate Officer
& Independent Marketing Consultant

"The path to successful entrepreneurship requires a significant personal contribution. "Starting Your Own Business" provides a handy, common-sense guide toward assessing one's ability to do what it takes to succeed."

Jay Schneider
Senior Architect
JBC Consulting, L.L.C.

I0475615

"Griff is one of the most gifted, passionate, and outstanding speakers I have ever heard. When I need the best advice about business, sales, and marketing, I call Griff!"

Tom Howe,
President
Legal Technology Group, Inc.

"A masterful book that combines unique self-assessment tools with personal wisdom and entrepreneurial knowledge that goes far beyond the traditional entrepreneurial text. Lindell's sound advice and practical know-how, built on sound entrepreneurial principles, is a must read for anyone starting or running a new business."

Dr. Deborah V. Brazeal
Cal Poly University, Pomona
Professor and Author

"Griff Lindell understands what it takes to succeed as an entrepreneur. By answering the questions found in this book—and understanding your own strengths and weaknesses—you may well be on your way to business success."

Gregg Mindt
Nonprofit Management Executive
The Mindt Group

"Griff's book provides a practical, yet tangible way to measure if you're ready to start a business and, if you're not, what specifically you need to do to improve your chances of success."

LD. "Spike" Bailey
Entrepreneur
LD Bailey & Associates

"As a business woman, I've found that time, support and passion are my key ingredients for success. Griff is right on target with these ten questions."

Marci Carvello
Character Collectibles

"This is a must read for the budding entrepreneur. Griff not only shows them how to see the apples in the seed, he also skillfully shows them how to plant, water, grow, and then harvest."

Jim Smith
Managing Partner
YCHANGE International

"The high percentage of failure for business start ups isn't just because of poor ideas, it's more about poor execution. Griff's common sense preview of the road faced by all entrepreneurs is a valuable - and economical - way to test the concept *before* investing the resources. This book can be a lifesaver if incorporated into your business plan."

Don Coley
Author/Non-profit Ministry Executive

Starting Your Own Business?
10 Questions to Consider *Before* Investing a Dime.

"I have never met a man with more passion for the entrepreneurial experience than Griff Lindell. He communicates with inspiration, clarity, and well-earned wisdom. For would-be entrepreneurs, this book will lead you on a journey of self discovery to help you decide if you have the desire and determination to start your own business."

Shannon Olson
Kennedy & Olson Advertising

"Concise and to the point. Not a lecture but a thorough in depth enjoyable read. Instant feedback with encouraging advice and simple points to ponder that most do not consider. Your best first investment. You owe it to yourself to read this book."

Dave Christoff
Entrepreneur, Hallmark Properties, Inc.

Starting Your Own Business?

10 Questions to Consider *Before* Investing a Dime.

P. Griffith Lindell

Elk Mountain Books, Wilsonville, Oregon

Starting Your Own Business?

P. Griffith Lindell

Published by:

Elk Mountain Books
PO Box 21
Wilsonville, Oregon 97070
info@elkmountianbooks.com

ISBN Print Edition: 1451547110
EAN-13: 9781451547115

Elk Mountain Books titles are available for special promotions and premiums. For details contact: sales@elkmountainbooks.com

Starting Your Own Business?
10 Questions to Consider *Before* Investing a Dime.

Table of Contents

About the Author

For more than twenty-five years, Certified Business Communicator P. Griffith (Griff) Lindell has served as a senior level marketing strategist and a leader to established, reorganizing, and emerging companies.

He has developed a unique process to assist executive teams in articulating their purpose, goals, core values, and strategy through customer-centric planning.

Using innovative and creative thinking tools, Griff shows budding entrepreneurs how to grasp an intimate understanding of customers, a thorough understanding of competitors, and a clearer understanding of themselves.

Griff has taught courses in leadership, sales, and marketing for such institutions as University of California, Azusa Pacific University, San Diego Christian College, Marylhurst University, and Concordia University.

As a motivational speaker, he has shared his unique insights on business with dozens of corporations including Medical Marketing Association; American Heart Association; Billy Graham Training Center; Business Marketing Association

(BMA); American Marketing Association; Hewlett Packard; Agilent; The Clorox Company, and Polycom International.

The author of more than a dozen business titles, he is currently an adjunct professor at universities in the Portland area, and volunteers as a SCORE counselor.

In his "spare time," Griff helped launch a charity providing homes, help and hope for displaced and distressed children of the world, beginning with an orphanage in Thailand (www.libertykidz.org).

When not writing or blogging, Griff is a motivational speaker, trainer, and provides consulting services to companies who want to expand their revenue and increase their impact through innovative thinking, compelling communications, and marketing strategies that have been proven effective time and again.

"Business success is good.
Personal Significance is what matters."
- Griff

Foreword

I had the great fortune to meet Griff Lindell two years into starting a high tech company.

His simple challenging questions (on which this book is centered) led to him becoming an invaluable resource for me.

Griff helped us with the successful positioning of our company and ultimately selling it three years later.

The questions in this book can be difficult to answer, and many entrepreneurs do not want to take the time or expend the brain cycles on these topics during the initial phase of starting a business.

It's easy to procrastinate - as there is never enough time.

Many dangerously believe the answers are obvious, or the answers are not important. Delaying addressing fundamental issues can lead to poor communication of core values and goals.

This book helps with the process.

Used wisely, it will help the reader address really important questions that, if not answered, could sabotage success.

Answering these questions, doing the assessment, using the note pages and journal could well become a "reality check" for you and your key staff when making difficult decisions.

Some years ago I wrote "No president or CEO should try to run a company without a Griff on their shoulder."

These questions, your answers, and your journaling process are the next best thing.

Read it.

Work it.

Use it.

Keep it on hand.

Both you and your business will benefit!

- Karen Milne

Karen Milne is a successful entrepreneur, who has spent 30 years in international high technology companies as well as several micro businesses.

She was a Co-Founder, President and CEO of Stardust Technologies, Inc. and Stardust.com (which was successfully sold to Penton Media in 1999); Co-Founder and COO of Aventail Corporation and Cofounder and EVP of cPower, Inc.

For all those brave hearts who are willing to launch out on their own and start a business.

Acknowledgments

To my fellow "retired" gang at Portland SCORE who have inspired me, invigorated me, and provided insights that in a large part, made this book possible.

Special thanks to Jim Smith, Kent Smith, Spike Bailey, Steve Senders, Steve Blanton, Sheila Bunnell, John Kuypers, Tim Thomas, David Hamacker, Tom Howe, Dick Mincheff and Bill Winton, SCORE colleagues all, who have encouraged me, held me accountable, and spent time reviewing my thoughts about small business when they first appeared on my blogs.

Thank you, Dick Fedchenko, for teaching me in words and deed. I appreciate your patience and persistence.

Thank you, son Paul, for being diligent that I connect with Perry P. Perkins whose editing, encouragement and execution of the publishing side made this book possible.

Thank you, Margaret Ann, my dear wife of over 40 years, for allowing me that time to just sit at my desk and think and write, who lovingly corrects my spelling, and willingly laughs at my bad jokes.

Thanks be to God my Creator, Redeemer and Friend. Any good thinking you see in this book is the result of my listening to Him; any bad thinking is all my own.

A Word from the Author

Finally, you have decided working for someone else is going to be part of your history.

You are going to work for *you*.

From the start, the process may have seemed like a 1000 piece puzzle, without the box, and with no picture of the final goal. Sure, you found the edge pieces, but it's all the other pieces scattered about that seem overwhelming.

You must consider the many aspects of running a business before you make the decision to invest in it.

> **Successful people ask better questions, and as a result, they get better answers. ~ Anthony Robbins**

The Chiropractor, Message Therapist, Computer Consultants, Auto Mechanic - you fill in the blank - who decides to open his or her own business, faces issues about which he or she may have little background training. Analyzing and fixing things (or people), they know. Bookkeeping, business processes, legalities, insurance, and the like, may be as foreign as an engine is to this author.

These may not be the *only* questions that you need to ask, but each of them will help you think about the business, family, emotional, and personal impact issues you will face.

They may even help you complete your new business puzzle.

How to use the
Activity & Notes Pages

I was taught that nothing happens until you write it down.

I ignored that advice when I was young – to my current dismay, and thought I could handle it without writing it out.

I was wrong. Writing it out is a discipline that helps our brains process information in a different way than just simply thinking about it. What works best is to not only make lists of things that need to be completed, but also to write notes about what was learned *as* those things were completed.

Here is an example – assume that you are buying a small, existing Auto Repair Shop:

Finished Activity Tracking

	Started	Completed
☐ I have penciled it out.	*March 1*	*March 30*

What I have learned:

March 1 – started working on my startup cost – discovered that I need to also figure in my business license costs with both the state and city.

March 3 – found out I had to set up a fictitious name for my business and then pay a business fee! The city wants fees too– ouch! – also learned that I have to have business insurance – talked to the bank about a business account – interesting conversation about what the bank will offer found out that I did not have some basic answers to equipment costs and code restrictions for my proposed shop.

	Started	Completed
☐ *Find out the code restrictions*	*March 3*	*March 5*

March 7 — worked on my location costs - discovered that building I was thinking about is not zoned for garages and there is no real parking available — will look for another location

March 8 - found location — good parking — but have some costs I had not anticipated with signage — the city does not allow me to put the sign up that was painted for me by Alan. they don't like the size .

Had a visit with Joyce about business insurance — all I want to do is fix cars - found out that I should also get disability for me since it's just me in the beginning — gotta protect Susie if I get hurt at my own shop — didn't think about that cost!

Started making a spreadsheet of my costs today…just keeping track of them is a major chore — I think what I need to do is spend about 10 min. each day collecting all the costs I've discovered.

For each item at the end of the chapter, you may discover that you will expand your "Things To Do List" quite a bit just as was done in this example:

	Started	Completed
Find out the code restrictions	*March 3*	*March 5*

Keeping track of those new items will help encourage you when the going gets tough because you can look back and see what you have accomplished.

The habit you form here could be live-changing.

I have a buddy who has been journaling for years about his business and has developed patterns of parts, labor, equipment and people that help him anticipate the future based on what has happened in the past.

Understanding his business history has protected him when times were tough and allowed him to expand more quickly than many of his competitors when times turned around.

Why? Because he recognized trends quickly. And you can too.

Start today.

Make a business diary.

Question #1
"Have you counted the costs?"

The old saying is that "it takes money to make money."

Starting your own business takes money.

The statistics are challenging - more than half of small businesses fail in their first year – after all that money has been spent by the entrepreneur for startup costs! Do you know where to find out how others are surviving in your new business category?

That sobering thought should stop many; but it doesn't. The "it won't happen to me" syndrome is alive and well for would-be entrepreneurs. That's expected.

You have a passion. A new idea. A belief that you can do something better. It drives you to take a risk. I understand.

But a "wise man considers the consequences ahead and PLANS for them. A fool goes blindly on and suffers the consequences" (*Proverbs*)

If you are single, you have only one person to worry about the potential loss of your savings.

However, if you have a family, of any number, you have a greater responsibility to others for the potential destruction of your financial situation.

So, in preparation for answering question #1, here are some other questions to consider:

A) Have you "penciled" the numbers?

- Can you sustain a business before it makes its first dollar?
- Can you make a profit with your potential revenue?
- Have you considered your startup costs and then your on-going monthly costs before revenue begins?

Once you have identified your startup costs, and your cash flow needs before you realize any revenue, you must then ask: "Do I have enough capital?" If not, add some!

B) Do you know what you need to break even (B-E), and when you will cross that magic line?

This graph will help you to determine your B-E point. This exercise is done, not just for your income, but also to find out how many "widgets" you have to sell each day to break even. If you are going to do a "Food Cart Business" how many sandwiches a day must you sell to break even?

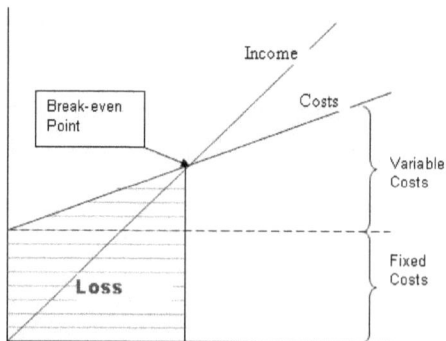

C) Are you hoping for investors?

- Do you have a plan for them to read?
- Does it show them how you make money?

How they will receive a return on their investment – that means getting their money back! Remember, all investors (banks, too) want their capital (original funds lent you) and interest on that money, coming to them in the future.

The **reality** is that most businesses receive their early financing with "friends and family money," and that, most often, comes after investing a good bit of their own.

When times are good, that money is often more available.

Now it is not. Banks are not the answer, neither are "angels" nor other investors – unless you can prove that your numbers are accurate, and you can support your concept with your own cash and credit invested. Get FREE help from seasoned people in the community (See SCORE in the Resources Appendix, to find help near you.)

There are other people in similar organizations within your local or state governments who can help you pencil out your idea, as well. See what the costs will be to start up. Assess the risks. Know the impact on you and your family.

Then, if the answers "line up," give it all you've got – *if* you're willing and able to bear great financial risk! Yes, I said "RISK." Success is not the miraculous, pie-in-the-sky, underdog story, that Hollywood makes it out to be. Sure, people risk and succeed, but many more risk and fail.

Don't be discouraged, but do go in with your eyes wide open, knowing that "miraculous success" is rare, but preparation and education can greatly increase the odds in your favor!

> **Trust in God, but tie your camel. ~ Persian Proverb**

Question 1 Assessment

Not yet   *Got it done!*

I have penciled it out.
1   2   3   4   5   6   7   8   9   10

I have money set aside.
1   2   3   4   5   6   7   8   9   10

I have access to money.
1   2   3   4   5   6   7   8   9   10

I have set up a cash flow forecast.
1   2   3   4   5   6   7   8   9   10

I know my start-up costs.
1   2   3   4   5   6   7   8   9   10

I have calculated my break-even point.
1   2   3   4   5   6   7   8   9   10

Add the numbers for your total: _____

54 – 60 = You are on your way!

48 – 53 = You are almost there – just a bit more work to do.

42 – 48 = Good start: know what's next and attack it.

41 or fewer = Are you sure you want to be in business?

Finished Activity Tracking

Started   *Completed*

☐ I have penciled it out.   _____   _____

What I have learned:

_____

_____

_____

_____

_____

_____

☐ I have money set aside.   _____   _____

What I have learned:

_____

_____

_____

_____

_____

_____

☐ **I have access to money.** _____ _____

What I have learned:

_____

_____

_____

_____

_____

_____

_____

☐ **I have set up a cash flow forecast.**

_____ _____

What I have learned:

_____

_____

_____

_____

_____

_____

_____

Starting Your Own Business?
10 Questions to Consider *Before* Investing a Dime.

	Started	*Completed*
☐ I know my start-up costs.	_____	_____

What I have learned:

_____

_____

_____

_____

_____

_____

_____

☐ I have calculated my break-even point.

_____   _____

What I have learned:

_____

_____

_____

_____

_____

_____

_____

☐ _____

                                    _____   _____

What I have learned:

_____

_____

_____

_____

_____

_____

_____

☐ _____

                                    _____   _____

What I have learned:

_____

_____

_____

_____

_____

_____

_____

10

Starting Your Own Business?
10 Questions to Consider *Before* Investing a Dime.

Started   *Completed*

☐ _____

                        _____   _____

What I have learned:

_____

_____

_____

_____

_____

_____

_____

☐ _____

                        _____   _____

What I have learned:

_____

_____

_____

_____

_____

_____

11

Question #2

"Are you ready, willing, and able for a change in your lifestyle?"

Your current lifestyle is probably a result of your career choice, the steady pay and benefits you receive, the vacation time you're granted and the other, softer benefits of your job.

Even if this is potentially "going away" because of *reduction in force* (RIF) or external changes in the marketplace, you have developed habit patterns based on your current job.

Becoming a small business owner changes most, if not all, of the attributes listed in that first sentence.

Vacations have a way of disappearing. The steady paycheck evaporates. Medical benefit packages may become complicated to get. Lifestyle, as you currently experience it, changes. However, perhaps the biggest change is your new workweek.

> **"By working faithfully for eight hours a day you may eventually get to be the boss and work twelve hours a day." ~ Robert Frost**

The beginning of a new enterprise is a black hole of time – entrepreneurs wear many hats and some of those hats must be worn when you are not in contact with your customers.

60 to 80-hour workweeks are not uncommon – you must give all to the cause, for all the details end up in *your* lap. You are the sales representative, the marketing person, the administration person, the janitor, the…well, you get the picture!

The other big change is your wages – that steady paycheck is a thing of the past. There have been many times in my start-up experiences when others had to be paid first, and I had to delay even my own, meager check.

How is your spouse going to feel about you not getting a paycheck when others are?

In fact, a livable salary often cannot be paid in the early years, and because you have started with your own funds, you are more likely to be drawing from your own well, rather than going to the new company's well.

The ever-present nature of the new business changes everything.

It is nearly impossible (or so it will seem) to find someone to do *your* job so you can "get away from it all."

Your laptop and cell phone (probably now a network connected device so you can always be in touch, no matter where you are) will become your constant companions.

You just cannot walk away from it any longer.

Being passionate about the idea can pay. You need to be "in touch" with that passion while you are developing a focused plan, daily managing and implementing that plan, and making the adjustments needed for external factors over which you have no control.

14

If you are willing to make a temporary lifestyle sacrifice, the end may be well worth the delay in gratification.

Build with the outcome in mind.

> **"The important thing is this: to be able at any moment to sacrifice what we are for what we could become." ~ Charles Du Bos**

Question 2 Assessment

Not yet   *Got it done.*

I have prepared myself and my family for a change in lifestyle.

1   2   3   4   5   6   7   8   9   10

I'm ready to work long hours.

1   2   3   4   5   6   7   8   9   10

I have the funds to pay my bills without drawing money from the new business.

1   2   3   4   5   6   7   8   9   10

I have written a business plan and my significant other has read it and understands the impact on our current lifestyle.

1   2   3   4   5   6   7   8   9   10

Add the numbers for your total: _____

36 – 40 = You are on your way!

32 – 35 = You are almost there – just a bit more work to do.

28 – 32 = Good start: know what's next and attack it.

27 or fewer = Are you sure you want to be in business?

Finished Activity Tracking

Started   *Completed*

☐ **I have prepared myself and my family for a change in
lifestyle.**

_____   _____

What I have learned:

_____

_____

_____

_____

_____

_____

☐ **I'm ready to work long hours.**   _____   _____

What I have learned:

_____

_____

_____

_____

_____

_____

☐ I have the funds to pay my bills without drawing money from the new business.

_____   _____

What I have learned:

_____

_____

_____

_____

_____

_____

☐ I have written a business plan and my significant other has read it and understands the impact on our current lifestyle.

_____   _____

What I have learned:

_____

_____

_____

_____

_____

_____

Starting Your Own Business?
10 Questions to Consider *Before* Investing a Dime.

Started   *Completed*

☐ _____

_____   _____

What I have learned:

_____
_____
_____
_____
_____
_____
_____

☐ _____

_____   _____

What I have learned:

_____
_____
_____
_____
_____
_____
_____

☐ _____

                                    _____   _____

What I have learned:

_____

_____

_____

_____

_____

_____

_____

☐ _____

                                    _____   _____

What I have learned:

_____

_____

_____

_____

_____

_____

_____

Question #3
"Is your support team on board?"

[Hang on here — this may be a bit heavy, but it is worth reading and meditating on its impact.]

"**All** mankind is of one author, and is one volume; when one man dies, one chapter is not torn out of the book, but translated into a better language; and every chapter must be so translated...

As therefore the bell that rings to a sermon, calls not upon the preacher only, but upon the congregation to come: so this bell calls us all: but how much more me, who am brought so near the door by this sickness...

No man is an island, [Emphasis added] entire of itself...any man's death diminishes me, because I am involved in mankind; and therefore never send to know for *whom the bell tolls; it tolls for thee.* [Emphasis added]" John Donne (1572-1631) Devotions Upon Emergent Occasions, Meditation XVII

Never truer is John Donne's observation about human nature than when you are deciding to become an entrepreneur.

Two concepts emerge in this famous Donne meditation: the interconnectedness of humans, and the impact of mortality:

In the life or death of a new enterprise, one may often find that one of its major causes was in the clear, considerate communication, or lack thereof, with your family.

The support of your loved ones is **vital** to your ability to sustain the energy, passion, and focus needed to plan your work and work your plan.

This will not be a short conversation; you must lay out, to the best of your current understanding, the potential impacts of your new time commitment, on their personal consumerism, and the sacrifices that you and they will need to make to see your new business vision become a reality.

Your family may not work in the business, but they are still connected to it because of **you**.

When you succeed, they succeed. If you fail, they have failed with you.

Therefore, talk seriously about the impact the new business will place on your time, your income, your lifestyle, your concentration and your family commitments. Rally the troops!

You will be in this venture TOGETHER.

The stress of devoting so much time and money to a new enterprise can threaten even strong relationships: weak ones – well, more stress, not less – at the least – will follow.

Help yourself succeed.

> **"There is no problem that can withstand the assault of sustained thinking."** ~Voltaire

How does this success process begin? Take personal time – each day - to think about what happened that day. What worked, what did not work?

It's time to start a business journal.

A very successful niche baker friend looks back at his journal notes often. It allows him to "be in the old moment" of what was happening to the marketplace and his feelings about it, his thoughts about what he might do, and actions he actually took.

He's not a writer, and the journal isn't pretty. The content, however, is critical.

Remembering the past, so we don't repeat our mistakes is a key to our future successes. Work at understanding what your competitors are saying to the market and what that might mean for you.

Is there an opportunity to differentiate your business in a new way?

Share your journal with your significant other, and make him or her part of the thought process, i.e. – "Here's what I am currently thinking: what do you think?"

Now is the time to think strategically and act tactically – and that flows from taking the time to understand what is happening on your city block, your section of town, your community, your customers, and your life.

Your support team can offer insights. Dialogue about these observations. Journal your reaction to them in light of the business you are starting. What gives meaning to understanding the customers you will be acquiring?

Get your support group on board!

Question 3 Assessment

Not yet   *Got it done.*

I have a general plan for my business future and I have the support of my spouse or significant other.
1   2   3   4   5   6   7   8   9   10

I have talked about my hopes, dreams and fears with my family.
1   2   3   4   5   6   7   8   9   10

I have talked over the finances with family.
1   2   3   4   5   6   7   8   9   10

I have written a business plan and my significant other has read it and understands the impact on our relationship.
1   2   3   4   5   6   7   8   9   10

Add the numbers for your total: _____

36 – 40 = You are on your way!

32 – 35 = You are almost there – just a bit more work to do.

28 – 32 = Good start: know what's next and attack it.

27 or fewer = Are you sure you want to be in business?

Finished Activity Tracking

Started   *Completed*

☐ I have a plan for my business future and I have the support of my spouse or significant other.

_____ _____

What I have learned:

_____

_____

_____

_____

_____

_____

☐ I have talked about my hopes, dreams and fears with my family.

_____ _____

What I have learned:

_____

_____

_____

_____

_____

_____

☐ I have talked over the finances with family.

                                         _____   _____

What I have learned:

_____

_____

_____

_____

_____

_____

☐ I have written a business plan and my significant other has read it and understands the impact on our relationship.

                                         _____   _____

What I have learned:

_____

_____

_____

_____

_____

_____

Starting Your Own Business?
10 Questions to Consider *Before* Investing a Dime.

Started   *Completed*

☐ _____

_____   _____

What I have learned:

_____

_____

_____

_____

_____

_____

_____

☐ _____

_____   _____

What I have learned:

_____

_____

_____

_____

_____

_____

_____

☐ _____

_____   _____

What I have learned:

_____

_____

_____

_____

_____

_____

_____

_____

☐ _____

_____   _____

What I have learned:

_____

_____

_____

_____

_____

_____

_____

Question #4
"Do you enjoy the business of business?"

You now have to decide: is this entrepreneurial idea just a hobby, or is it really a business?

Moreover…do you *enjoy* the business of business?

In the beginning, you do it all for the business, and one of the most important items that you must tackle is **writing the business plan.**

Few have training in that area. The good news is there are plenty of community organizations that can help – again, you can find one of the best at SCORE. You will find free counseling and reasonably priced workshops that will teach you how to write a plan.

Cash is KING when running a small business, but I have discovered that many, who have been in business for several years, and now are struggling, have never done a **cash flow forecast**.

Learn to love Excel®, for it will help you with managing cash.

Quicken® is great for bookkeeping, but not for a month-to-month moving cash analysis.

One of the most inexpensive, yet powerful programs is found at www.scorepdx.org, and is well worth the price.

By the way, if it seems like I'm a huge fan of SCORE…it's because I am! SCORE is a resource for entrepreneurs and small business owners looking to achieve success. They provide free counseling from business people who "have been there and done that," workshops, and valuable resources to help you start and/or run your small business.

Prospects need to know about your business, and you need to know what these potential customers want, how they are currently meeting those needs, and how to attract them to your offering.

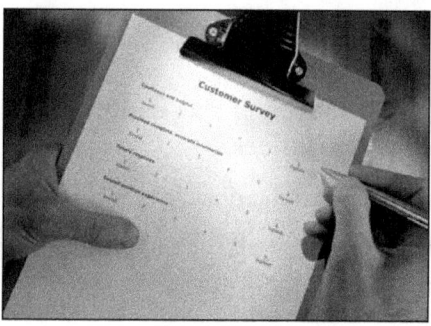

This demands some **_market research_** to make these discoveries.

This can be fun, if you enjoy looking, learning, asking questions, and listening to what is said…_and_ what is left out of, the answer.

People are willing to share if they know you are sincere and want to learn. For under a hundred bucks, you can find out how others are doing in the same business.

Discover:

- How much revenue they are generating

- How many are located in your marketing area.

- How much they generate per square foot, or per employee.

All of this information is at your fingertips, if you just know where to get it.

Many with whom I have chatted about starting a new business have no idea who is doing something in the market that mirrors or matches what they want to do. Learn from their successes and failures.

And, after you have collected your data about whom is doing what and why, THEN you can set about writing **compelling marketing communications** – flyers, the back of your business cards, signs, ads, websites, blogs, tweets, etc.

> **"I don't care how much power, brilliance or energy you have, if you don't harness it and focus it on a specific target, and hold it there, you're never going to accomplish as much as your ability warrants."**
> **~ Zig Ziglar**

Remember, given the right information you must know "who is my customer, and where can I find them?"

You also have to know what will compel these people to buy from you.

When you start that new business, you are responsible for crafting the messages: as you grow, you can hire talent to hone those messages for you and focus them on each of kinds of marketing communications you need.

Sales- that "awful" word. No one likes to be sold to, but they love to buy! Selling is a must for the early stage entrepreneur: after all…

Nothing happens until someone sells something!

Your fear of and misconceptions about selling may get in the way of your success.

Learning how to ask questions, understand the problem, and then offer your solution is a process that all can master – you don't have to be a "master salesperson" to get started.

Hiring, managing, and firing - at some point, you have to begin to multiply yourself.

Learning how to hire carefully, managing by training, trust, and teaching, can will help you in not having to face the other "T" – termination.

Nevertheless, you do have to learn! Community colleges often have workshops to help.

Asking people for money - investment money – is hard for many people, simply because one instinctively knows the potential investor will ask the "hard" questions.

When you ask for investment money or a bank loan, those people want to see your passion, but they also want to know your purpose and plans.

You, not someone you hire, has to write that business plan, so you can ask for that needed capital based on your understanding of the market, and your unique offering. You must be able to explain why it is so special, how it is unlike others, and what kind of money you need to become a success.

The person or organization that you ask to invest will want to know what you will be spending their investment on, and how you will achieve a return on that investment.

If you don't *own* your numbers, they will quickly see that you don't know this information. Someone else has written the plan, and they will want to talk to *that* person because it is *that* person who really knows the business – not you.

Balancing the checkbook – a simple task, but often neglected (*see Cash Flow page 33*) If you have sloppy habits in personally managing your bank account, they will only be magnified for your small business.

Personally, I found it time-consuming to subtract the check from the carrying balance each time: but I did learn, early on, that to succeed, I must bring the checkbook balance up to date *every night.*

Pay your bills – on time…every time.

Excuses like "I'm just too busy" don't cut it.

Remember that commitment of time we wrote about in answering question #2? This is one place where you *must* invest your time, looking at terms offered and scheduling the payments accordingly.

2% Net 10 – is a great deal for you: do you take advantage of it? (See Resources) Making that schedule visible, so you are not forgetting to look at it each day, is vital.

Organize. Organize. Organize. If you just find this too hard to do, get someone to help…or scrap the whole idea…it's *that* important!

> **"While we keep a man waiting, he reflects on our shortcomings." ~ French Proverb**

Being late can affect much more of your business today than you can ever know. It can increase your insurance rates, the price your vendors charge you (your price discounts), your credit card's available balance, and much, much more.

Pay on time and your financial "word" gets much stronger, much quicker!

Confront people who don't pay their bills – This is the flip side of managing the money. There are times when you have to do this quickly, firmly, and with civility.

Don't make enemies. Make money.

Also, make certain that you have a credit policy! How much credit you're going to extend to each customer, and why?

Be certain, if you are going to extend credit, that you extend it only to those who are *credit worthy.*

Have your banker help you with some of the things that you need to look at to decide who is worthy of your credit.

When one of these folks doesn't pay their bill on time, *don't* extend more credit: GET PAID FIRST. It's not a sale until you have collected the money. Don't put it off. It will not get better on its own. Work out a payment plan.

If you have to, go to small claims court. Collect your debts.

Negotiating – the process of buying from others and reselling, or the process of selling service to others, both require good negotiating skills.

There are programs, courses, and blogs on this art – learn it, and learn to enjoy doing it.

Enjoying the process is part of the solution for success in the doing of it. I know. I hated negotiating at one time. However, I had to learn to distinguish myself from the process, and to focus on the outcome. I had to learn to love it!

There are others issues, as well…forming the company and its legal status, business insurance, accounting, endgame plan, and much more.

I have not said much about the "thing" that you want to do in your business, i.e. the *thing* that is your passion.

The activity, or product, that awoke that entrepreneurial spirit still has to be nurtured, managed, and expressed – but if you don't pay attention to these business issues, you simply have a hobby.

Hobbies are okay…good to have, in fact.

They are *not* a business.

Question 4 Assessment

Not yet   *Got it done.*

I have a written business plan.
1   2   3   4   5   6   7   8   9   10

If YES, my plan has been reviewed by an objective third party.
1   2   3   4   5   6   7   8   9   10

I understand the principles of cash flow.
1   2   3   4   5   6   7   8   9   10

I have a cash flow tool (Excel software or the like).
1   2   3   4   5   6   7   8   9   10

I have done market research, even at a rudimentary level.
1   2   3   4   5   6   7   8   9   10

I have scoped out the competition, and understand their value proposition.
1   2   3   4   5   6   7   8   9   10

I have worked on my sales skills.
1   2   3   4   5   6   7   8   9   10

I have written my "elevator speech*" so I can effectively talk to potential investors.
1   2   3   4   5   6   7   8   9   10

I have a bookkeeper or a bookkeeping system.
1   2   3   4   5   6   7   8   9   10

I have worked on my negotiating skills.
1   2   3   4   5   6   7   8   9   10

Add the numbers for your total: _____

90-100 = You are on your way!

80-89 = You are almost there – just a bit more work to do.

70-79 = Good start: know what's next and attack it.

69 or fewer = Are you sure you are ready to be in business?

---

*An elevator speech, or *elevator pitch*, is a short and persuasive speech about a product, service, or project. Good elevator pitches are concise, compelling, and tightly focused to their target audience.

As the name reflects, the idea is that the entire pitch should be delivered in the time span as an elevator ride, approximately thirty seconds to two minutes. See page 72 for a more detailed explanation of how to write this pitch.

For my free eReport on creating an elevator speech:

"Explaining Your Business So People "Get It!"

Email me at: griff@lindellassociates.net

Finished Activity Tracking

Started   *Completed*

☐ I have a written business plan.

——————   ——————

What I have learned:

_____

_____

_____

_____

_____

_____

☐ My business plan has been reviewed by an objective
   third party.

——————   ——————

What I have learned:

_____

_____

_____

_____

_____

_____

41

☐ I understand the principles of cash flow.

_____   _____

What I have learned:

_____

_____

_____

_____

_____

_____

_____

☐ I have a cash flow tool.

_____   _____

What I have learned:

_____

_____

_____

_____

_____

_____

_____

Starting Your Own Business?
10 Questions to Consider *Before* Investing a Dime.

Started   *Completed*

☐ I have done market research, even at a
  rudimentary level.

_____   _____

What I have learned:

_____

_____

_____

_____

_____

_____

_____

☐ I have scoped out the competition, and understand
  their value proposition.

_____   _____

What I have learned:

_____

_____

_____

_____

_____

_____

_____

☐ I have worked on my sales skills.

                                     _____   _____

What I have learned:

_____

_____

_____

_____

_____

_____

_____

☐ I have written my "elevator speech" so I can effectively talk to potential investors.

                                     _____   _____

What I have learned:

_____

_____

_____

_____

_____

_____

_____

Started   *Completed*

☐ I have a bookkeeper or a bookkeeping system.

_____   _____

What I have learned:

_____

_____

_____

_____

_____

_____

_____

☐ I have worked on my negotiating skills.

_____   _____

What I have learned:

_____

_____

_____

_____

_____

_____

_____

Started   *Completed*

☐ _____

_____   _____

What I have learned:

_____

_____

_____

_____

_____

_____

_____

☐ _____

_____   _____

What I have learned:

_____

_____

_____

_____

_____

_____

_____

Starting Your Own Business?
10 Questions to Consider *Before* Investing a Dime.

	Started	*Completed*
☐ _____		
	_____	_____

What I have learned:

_____

_____

_____

_____

_____

_____

_____

| ☐ _____ | | |
| | _____ | _____ |

What I have learned:

_____

_____

_____

_____

_____

_____

_____

Question #5
"Are you comfortable making decisions on the fly?

Mountain climbing is about the route, standard holds, steps, swings, and ways to get to the top.

Once a particular route is completed, you may take it a second time for "practice."

Owning a small business, on the other hand, is more like Ice climbing. The route you take up the "frozen falls" changes with every season.

There is no route-guide.

There is no guide-book on which way to the top is most or least challenging. Every season, it's all new. The decisions you make on your way up to the top may have some fundamental basis to them, but they are each an individual application of some basic principle.

It's the same with running a small business. The buck stops with you in a way you may have never before experienced when you were working for someone else. In your new small business, you assume full responsibility for what happens day-by-day. Every inch up the "falls" is your own unique route. This new state of affairs – no corporate "play-book" – changes everything. Previously, the "boss" made the decisions in your company, and those were most often from a playbook and/or significant training on thinking and decision-making processes, which you were not privy to.

Even if you were a Supervisor, Manager, Director, C-level, you always had *someone* to report to, and be accountable to.

You also had someone to turn to for guidance; you had a team, sometimes, who could debate possible decision consequences, helping you see what was the good, better, or best decision.

This is no longer true. You are on your own now. *You* have to make all of the decisions, and there will be many to make.

In the "Do You Enjoy the Business of Business" chapter, we touched on many of the fundamental business issues which must be understood and addressed, but not all of the possible variations of them.

Often, the issues about which you must decide come at you "fast and furious" – think again of climbing that frozen water fall. The route decisions will be made from the foundation of your preparation. Prepare well – decide well.

> **"Listening, not imitation, may be the sincerest form of flattery."** ~ **Dr Joyce Brothers**

Research has shown that successful entrepreneurs seem to have that ability to make decisions and actually love the process – they have learned how to **listen – really listen.**

Your customers, your vendors, your peers, and your competitors…are all talking. Are you hearing what they are saying - especially your customers? Often it is the off-handed comments from a faithful customer that will help you clarify the *mission* for your business. Sometimes their comments can drive innovation...*if*...you are listening, learning and leveraging the ideas that emerge.

Successful entrepreneurs, especially, have the ability to make decisions involving risk, because they have prepared themselves well. They have not only thought about customers, markets, competitors, finances, and business issues, but they have written them down in some form, and so risk management is better handled.

The risks take on new meaning because they fit within a *context*, so you can more readily identify those elements of risks that emerge. Because of your preparation, you will be better able to assesses them, and prioritize the management of your resources to meet them.

"Managing on the fly" does not mean you develop a dashboard to survive and thrive. Actually, managing without a play-book means that you develop your own "dashboard dials" to help make decisions.

You would not drive a vehicle without a gas gauge, so why would you try to drive your business without a "business" fuel gauge?

Do you know how much it will cost for you to open your doors each day? How much "business fuel" you need to keep your business engine running for a day, a week, a month?

You are in a new world. One that will stimulate you in new ways. The future is muddy and murky, but you still must sometimes muddle through.

You can do this better if you have a clear picture of what has happened (how much gas has been used); what your present situation is (how much gas is left, and how far to the next station), and what your future could be. Don't race at stop lights...conserve fuel – slow down a bit – coast to an obvious red light.

The word *entrepreneur* means, "enter new" and you, along with most small businesses are doing just that – entering new "territory." Entrepreneurs thrive on collecting data, analyzing it, and choosing a path – even one that involves risk. Risk is not a monolithic concept – it is on a continuum, and every decision you make involves a varying degree of it.

> **"First ask yourself: What is the worst that can happen? Then prepare to accept it. Then proceed to improve on the worst." ~ Dale Carnegie**

Still, not all decisions are venturing into the unknown – many demand analysis of facts that are already available, but have to be sought out – which takes time, effort, and thought.

Not putting in the "work" first, presents a risk of a different sort – the "bad" kind that could lead to failure. One piece of preparation is the business plan.

In your business plan, you made some assumptions based on your educated analysis of market conditions, your ability to attract and retain customers in the existing market, and even acquiring customers from new and different markets. Now, you are doing something – working the plan. Something *happens*...you get a *result*.

Now you must record that result (always journal – even if it's only bullet points), analyze it by comparing the results to the plan, and then evaluate the variances from the old plan to form a new plan given these results.

The new "state of affairs" means that, often, you don't have the luxury of time, or staff, to work the process. It happens in real time, and it's all about you.

Get comfortable with it.

Real-time decisions are the rule, not the exception. Thinking on the fly. Thinking quickly. Making decisions.

Now, you're in business…you gotta love it!

Question 5 Assessment

Not yet   *Got it done.*

I have proven that I can make tough decisions.
1   2   3   4   5   6   7   8   9   10

I have thought through what will be different for me working without a team beside me.
1   2   3   4   5   6   7   8   9   10

I have demonstrated in my life that I can think "on the fly."
1   2   3   4   5   6   7   8   9   10

I have proven that I can work without a structured process.
1   2   3   4   5   6   7   8   9   10

Add the numbers for your total: _____

36 – 40 = You are on your way!

32 – 35 = You are almost there – just a bit more work to do.

28 – 32 = Good start: know what's next and attack it.

27 or fewer = Are you sure you want to be in business?

Finished Activity Tracking

Started   Completed

☐ I have proven that I can make tough decisions.

_____   _____

What I have learned:

_____

_____

_____

_____

_____

_____

_____

☐ I have thought through what will be different for me working without a team beside me.

_____   _____

What I have learned:

_____

_____

_____

_____

_____

_____

_____

☐ I have demonstrated that I can think "on the fly."

                                        —————   —————

What I have learned:

_____

_____

_____

_____

_____

_____

_____

_____

☐ I have proven that I can work without a structured process.

                                        —————   —————

What I have learned:

_____

_____

_____

_____

_____

_____

_____

_____

Starting Your Own Business?
10 Questions to Consider *Before* Investing a Dime.

Started   *Completed*

☐ _____

_____   _____

What I have learned:

_____

_____

_____

_____

_____

_____

_____

☐ _____

_____   _____

What I have learned:

_____

_____

_____

_____

_____

_____

_____

☐ _____

_____   _____

What I have learned:

_____
_____
_____
_____
_____
_____
_____

☐ _____

_____   _____

What I have learned:

_____
_____
_____
_____
_____
_____
_____

Question #6
"What's your track record of making stuff happen?"

Ideas have power.

An organized, synthesized, and focused idea - driven toward implementation - is the fuel of strategy.

You have shown from experience that, not only can you generate ideas, but you also know how to actually "get stuff done" with them.

The "stuff" you want to get done is a goal.

Write them down. Check them off when completed.

Make certain that this "stuff" is clearly identified and is short-term — so you have a real chance of completing the goal; attainable — not "pie in the sky, by and by" but real goals that will help you exercise the power of your idea; and make them *measurable* — "by a certain date, or after a certain event, such and such will happen."

Keep your objective in clear view and be:

Continually preparing – like ice climbing, each hold, each step, is a preparation for the next – hang on, relax, keep climbing.

Consistently focused – ideas that have power are crisp, and easily understood. The implementation may have some fuzziness to the actual steps that will be taken, but the goal is clear.

Completely committed – without a firm commitment to a move as you are climbing, you are in deep trouble. Belief and commitment are a matter of the will – even when the move is uncertain.

The goal, and the path your take to it, are clear, your belief, with all your focus and energy, can make the difference between attainment and sliding back.

> **"There are risks and costs to a program of action. But they are far less than the long-range risks and costs of comfortable inaction." ~ John F. Kennedy**

Strategy formulation is often the grist of many company meetings.

The power that makes a difference in a firm's success is derived from the *implementation* of the plan – *not* in formulating the plan.

The valley between the peak of your great business idea and the peak of marketplace acceptance is huge. The cliffs are shear. Many people make it to the top of the peak of ideas, but unfortunately, research indicates that few know how to navigate from that peak to the peak of performance.

So, how do you know if you have what it takes to bridge that gap?

One way is to look, again, at your history:

- Did you show implementation skills in your childhood? You executed on making your own version of "the lemonade stand." Maybe, you figured out how to sell cookies for an organization, an idea that was praised for its new approach.

- You might have successfully run for school office, presenting useful ideas that students and teachers could both support.

- Perhaps, you loved sports and often led, even without the title of captain.

- You helped organize and implement class projects.

- You lead a study group in college.

- At work, you are often the first one in, and the last one out - you get stuff done.

Your history is painted with the brush of **the go-to person.**

It is these kinds of behaviors that distinguish successful entrepreneurs from all others. They get stuff done. They take an idea (theirs, someone else's, it does not matter) and execute it, and they are always looking for way to execute *better* - always talking to customers about their experiences, and looking for ways to improve.

Plan your work.

Work your plan.

Talk to people in similar businesses about how they got started, the impediments to moving forward, and the issues that they discovered…but wished they had known earlier.

Executing your plan has now begun.

Question 6 Assessment

Not yet   *Got it done.*

I have developed a strategic plan based on ideas that I have "tested" in the real world.

| 1 | 2 | 3 | 4 | 5 | 6 | 7 | 8 | 9 | 10 |

I have developed an implementation time-line with benchmarks to keep track of progress.

| 1 | 2 | 3 | 4 | 5 | 6 | 7 | 8 | 9 | 10 |

I have a history of idea generation, and have thought about what I have learned, so that I can apply it to my new business idea.

| 1 | 2 | 3 | 4 | 5 | 6 | 7 | 8 | 9 | 10 |

I have collaborated with people who have started businesses similar to mine.

| 1 | 2 | 3 | 4 | 5 | 6 | 7 | 8 | 9 | 10 |

Add the numbers for your total: _____

36 – 40 = You are on your way!

32 – 35 = You're almost there – just a bit more work to do.

28 – 32 = Good start: know what's next and attack it.

27 or fewer = Are you sure you want to be in business?

Finished Activity Tracking

☐ **I have developed a strategic plan based on ideas that I have "tested" in the real world.**

_____   _____

What I have learned:

_____

_____

_____

_____

_____

_____

_____

☐ **I have developed an implementation timeline with benchmarks to keep track of progress.**

_____   _____

What I have learned:

_____

_____

_____

_____

_____

_____

_____

Started   *Completed*

☐ I have a history of idea generation, and have thought about what I have learned, so I can apply it to my new business idea.

_____   _____

What I have learned:

_____

_____

_____

_____

_____

_____

_____

☐ I have collaborated with people who have started businesses similar to mine.

_____   _____

What I have learned:

_____

_____

_____

_____

_____

_____

_____

☐ _____

_____   _____

What I have learned:

_____

_____

_____

_____

_____

_____

_____

☐ _____

_____   _____

What I have learned:

_____

_____

_____

_____

_____

_____

_____

Starting Your Own Business?
10 Questions to Consider *Before* Investing a Dime.

	Started	*Completed*
☐ _____		
	_____	_____

What I have learned:

_____

_____

_____

_____

_____

_____

_____

| ☐ _____ | | |
| | _____ | _____ |

What I have learned:

_____

_____

_____

_____

_____

_____

_____

Question #7
"How well do you communicate?"

Communicating is different than speaking.

Some people are adequate public speakers, and yet not gifted communicators – who often have the ability to motivate change, inspire, and drive action.

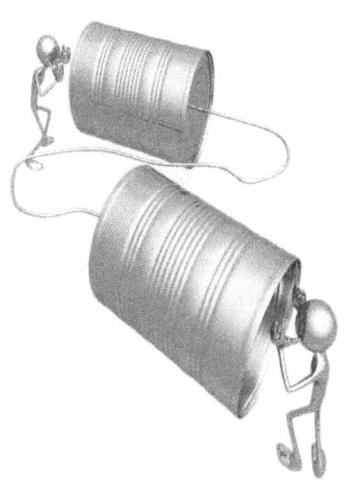

Entrepreneurs need to be great communicators.

This communication process begins with you. *You* must have a clear picture of what you want to say and why it is of value.

You must have a clear understanding of exactly what it is that you want to communicate. Whether you are explaining your product or service, your business, your unique advantage and why you deliver the best value, or are just chatting to establish rapport, preparation is 80% of the battle – even before you open your mouth.

How does this happen?

I have often said, "it isn't real until you write it down." That's one reason writing a business plan is so important.

It prepares you to communicate.

> **"By failing to prepare, you are preparing to fail."**
> **~ Benjamin Franklin**

When crafting your business plan, those closest to you want to hear that you are able to communicate the following:

- **Passion** - a riveting enthusiasm that is born from your understanding of the marketplace, the potential customer needs, the way you will meet that need, and why you are in a good position to succeed at meeting that need.

- **Purpose** - your purpose in life with this business - why this is more than just a hobby – this will be a business that has a *future*, that you have thought about what you want to do with your business in six months, three years, and even further into the future; and…

- **Plans** – not the actual business plan that you unfold and share – rather, your listeners want to feel comfortable that you actually have a plan with milestones, goals to accomplish, and changes you want to make in the way that this particular business is done.

As you are developing that plan, working with others to hone it, and digging into understanding what currently drives the market and how you will participate in that drive, or change it, your plan gives you the knowledge needed to become a *communicator* about your business.

Have you noticed how people often can be "persuasive and well–spoken" about their hobby. Their eyes brighten. Their posture changes. Their cadence is quicker and energized.

All of these are elements of communication, and the first steps to effective persuasion.

Transferring those natural skills to a business setting is sometimes hindered by roadblocks in our thinking, roadblocks that need to be overcome.

Joining an organization like Toastmasters, for example, will help you develop the comfort level needed to improve your communication skills - the skills you need to develop or hone when talking about - well, almost anything!

Here are some hints to help, if you find yourself having to actually speak at a business club, meeting, or in front of any group...

1. Only you know who you are, so always write your own introduction.

2. The first 30 seconds is "do or die" – capture their interest or lose the audience.

3. Too shallow, too deep, or juuussst right – you can't tell them everything in 30 minutes – so just tell them the one or two most important things.

4. Don't try to sell anything, just communicate passion, purpose and plans.

5. Include a Q&A session – it's not as formal, and can be a lot of fun.

6. Always exit through a trap door, trailing fire, and singing "The Star Spangled Banner" – in other words, end with a bang – not just a thank you

Developing a powerful elevator pitch drives your effective business communication.

Writing that pitch, sweating over each word and phrase, honing it, and reading it aloud over and over again, will allow you, in a conversation, to communicate naturally.

The elements of that pitch include:

- The target audience – who is this customer? What common characteristics do they share, what common values drive them, and what other attributes do they possess to be *your* target market?

- What do they need – have you determined *their* needs? Do *they* even know their needs? (They may not, if what you are offering is something new.)

- What you offer – simply the name of your business or product.

- What it is so very special about your offering – this is your *statement of value* – your unique selling advantage, and the greatest benefit you deliver.

- How it is unlike other offerings in the same market space? Do you know how their needs are being met now, and how you are meeting them in a different way? What are the attributes that distinguish *you*?

Of course, this pitch is not fiction: it is borne from analysis of yourself, your industry, your market, your typical customer, your competition, and your offering (product or service).

Persuasion is most often a result of knowledge, understanding, and communicating the value of your new business offering.

No one buys features: people respond to value!

Capture the passion you have about your hobby, and transfer those communication skills to your new venture. Then, you will better communicate both your ideas, and why they are of *value* to customers.

Question 7 Assessment

Not yet   *Got it done.*

I have displayed an ability to communicate well.
1   2   3   4   5   6   7   8   9   10

I know who my target markets are for my product or service.
1   2   3   4   5   6   7   8   9   10

I have identified what motivates them to buy.
1   2   3   4   5   6   7   8   9   10

I have matched those needs to what I will offer.
1   2   3   4   5   6   7   8   9   10

I have identified what is unique or special about my offering (product or service).
1   2   3   4   5   6   7   8   9   10

I can clearly differentiate my offering from the competition.
1   2   3   4   5   6   7   8   9   10

I have developed a list of attributes that make what I'm selling different and compelling.
1   2   3   4   5   6   7   8   9   10

I have developed my pitch.

1   2   3   4   5   6   7   8   9   10

I have said my pitch aloud at least 40 times.

1   2   3   4   5   6   7   8   9   10

I am comfortable, in a casual conversation, telling people what I do and how it will benefit them.

1   2   3   4   5   6   7   8   9   10

Add the numbers for your total: _____

90-100 = You are on your way!

80-89 = You are almost there – just a bit more work to do.

70-79 = Good start: know what's next and attack it.

69 or fewer = Are you sure you are ready to be in business?

Finished Activity Tracking

Started   *Completed*

☐ **I have displayed an ability to communicate well.**

_____   _____

What I have learned:

_____

_____

_____

_____

_____

_____

_____

☐ **I know who my target markets are for my product or service.**

_____   _____

What I have learned:

_____

_____

_____

_____

_____

_____

_____

☐ **I have identified what motivates my target markets to buy.**

_____   _____

What I have learned:

_____

_____

_____

_____

_____

_____

_____

☐ **I have matched those needs to what I will offer.**

_____   _____

What I have learned:

_____

_____

_____

_____

_____

_____

_____

_____

_____

Starting Your Own Business?
10 Questions to Consider *Before* Investing a Dime.

Started   *Completed*

☐ **I have identified what is unique or special about my offering (product or service).**

_____   _____

What I have learned:

_____

_____

_____

_____

_____

_____

_____

☐ **I can clearly differentiate my offering from the competition.**

_____   _____

What I have learned:

_____

_____

_____

_____

_____

_____

_____

☐ **I have developed a list of attributes that make what I'm selling different and compelling.**

_____   _____

What I have learned:

_____

_____

_____

_____

_____

_____

☐ **I have developed my pitch.**

_____   _____

What I have learned:

_____

_____

_____

_____

_____

_____

Started   *Completed*

☐ **I have said my pitch aloud at least 40 times.**

_____ _____

What I have learned:

_____

_____

_____

_____

_____

_____

_____

☐ **I am comfortable in a casual conversation, telling people what I do and how it will benefit them.**

_____ _____

What I have learned:

_____

_____

_____

_____

_____

_____

☐ _____

_____   _____

What I have learned:

_____

_____

_____

_____

_____

_____

☐ _____

_____   _____

What I have learned:

_____

_____

_____

_____

_____

_____

Starting Your Own Business?
10 Questions to Consider *Before* Investing a Dime.

	Started	*Completed*
☐ _____		
	_____	_____

What I have learned:

_____

_____

_____

_____

_____

_____

_____

☐ _____

_____   _____

What I have learned:

_____

_____

_____

_____

_____

_____

_____

Question #8

"Is this new business something about which you are passionate?"

Passion fuels us. Without passion for a business category, or industry, the small businessperson will have a tough go of it.

Ryan Hoback, writing at Motivated Entrepreneur, expresses it this way:

> *"I live to create....I eat, sleep, walk and talk about innovation, creativity and new business. When I get excited about a new venture that I have been developing, I feel the excitement run deep through my body.*
>
> *A feeling of invigoration comes across me.*
>
> *When a new idea comes to my mind, I begin to get happy like a little child opening a present on their birthday. You see, this is passion, and this is what successful business organizations are built on. Passion.*
>
> *Passion is the driving force and inner desire among entrepreneurs and leaders across the world which makes you want to continually pursue going above and beyond."*

Starting a business demands that energy, that *passion*.

The "day-to-dayness" of starting and running a new business, especially when you are struggling with all the aspects of a business for which you may not be well equipped, can be overwhelming.

83

> **"Each of us has a fire in our heart for something.
> It's our goal in life to find it and to keep it lit."
> ~ Mary Lou Retton**

Without passion, you may easily let the important details slide and only focus on one small aspect of the business that you enjoy. Not good for you, really. Certainly not good for the business.

Passion is not a substitute for business understanding or even intelligence. Passion cannot replace product knowledge, positioning strategy, or planning excellence. Nevertheless, without *passion*, each of those qualities is like a loosely tied balloon – the air leaks out, and it quickly goes flat.

Tom Peters pointed out in his ground-breaking book *In Search of Excellence*, "Nothing good or great can be done in the absence of enthusiasm."

It's the knot which holds the air in the balloon.

Passion is what will help you discipline yourself to get up early, work late, learn new business practices, work with cranky customers, collect past-due money, and begin all over the next day...often doing the same things.

Passion is a choice, and it must become your daily choice. No matter how you feel physically, no matter how the economy fares, no matter how tired you may be...you must choose to set those feelings aside and be passionate about your new pursuit!

If this idea seems strange, extraordinarily difficult, or even completely foreign to you, you may want to consider finding a job – and not creating a career.

Starting Your Own Business?
10 Questions to Consider *Before* Investing a Dime.

Successful entrepreneurs are passionate about their businesses, and customers know it, love it, and continue coming back to those business owners that love the process.

Need help with your practice, your purpose, your products...your "passion?"

Contact us at Lindell Associates, LLC.

Lindell Associates, LLC exists to provide compelling consulting, facilitating, coaching, training and mentoring services, focused on both small business and teams within larger organization.

Our approach is grounded in customer-centric thinking (looking at your brand from the customer's perspective) and servant-leadership principles.

See Resources *for more information on Lindell Associates.*

Question 8 Assessment

Not yet   *Got it done.*

I stay as fit as possible to keep my energy up.
1   2   3   4   5   6   7   8   9   10

I understand my product or service category to a high degree.
1   2   3   4   5   6   7   8   9   10

I have developed a positioning strategy.
1   2   3   4   5   6   7   8   9   10

I have developed a personal purpose statement.
1   2   3   4   5   6   7   8   9   10

I have developed a purpose statement for my business.
1   2   3   4   5   6   7   8   9   10

I have a method to remind me that "passion is a choice."
1   2   3   4   5   6   7   8   9   10

Add the numbers for your total: _____

54 – 60 = You are on your way!

48 – 53 = You are almost there – just a bit more work to do.

42 – 48 = Good start: know what's next and attack it.

41 or fewer = Are you sure you want to be in business?

Finished Activity Tracking

Started   *Completed*

☐ **I stay fit as possible to keep my energy up.**

_____   _____

What I have learned:

_____

_____

_____

_____

_____

_____

☐ **I understand the product or service category to a high degree.**

_____   _____

What I have learned:

_____

_____

_____

_____

_____

_____

☐ **I have developed a positioning strategy.**

                                                      _____   _____

What I have learned:

_____

_____

_____

_____

_____

_____

_____

☐ **I have developed a personal purpose statement.**

                                                      _____   _____

What I have learned:

_____

_____

_____

_____

_____

_____

_____

Started   *Completed*

☐ I have developed a purpose statement for my business.

_____   _____

What I have learned:

_____

_____

_____

_____

_____

_____

☐ I have a method to remind me that "passion is a choice."

_____   _____

What I have learned:

_____

_____

_____

_____

_____

_____

☐ _____

       _____   _____

What I have learned:

_____

_____

_____

_____

_____

_____

_____

☐ _____

       _____   _____

What I have learned:

_____

_____

_____

_____

_____

_____

_____

Starting Your Own Business?
10 Questions to Consider *Before* Investing a Dime.

Started   *Completed*

☐ _____

_____   _____

What I have learned:

_____

_____

_____

_____

_____

_____

_____

☐ _____

_____   _____

What I have learned:

_____

_____

_____

_____

_____

_____

_____

Question #9

"Are you a person that gives others Energy – A self-starter?"

Let's be honest - starting a business can be a discouraging journey.

You may find that the world does not respond as you would.

You return phone calls. You answer email. You help people when they ask for help.

You look at the blank screen, the blank piece of paper, as a challenge, not an obstacle.

YOU are an indefatigable person of energy and initiative.

If that paragraph in some way describes you, then be encouraged! You have a chance of success in starting a business. If you can combine persistence with the right kind of impatience, you are on the road to success.

You are *results* oriented. You don't look at life as a choice between success and failure.

You understand that actions produce results.

If you don't like the result, you change what was done so you produce a different result.

A self-starter lives and learns…and then learns some more.

Negative results spur change. Exciting changes. It's not about the result - it is about what you are learning from that result. Always learn.

What to do. What not to do.

Innovators constantly produce results that do not match the goal – each result demonstrates something that did not help achieve the goal so they change what is done to produce a different result.

A **results** paradigm, rather than a *success-failure* paradigm builds a positive attitude within you.

> "Things turn out best for the people who make the best out of the way things turn out." ~Art Linkletter

Nurture a Positive Attitude. People are attracted to people who are quietly confident and positive. No one likes a whiner – not even *your psyche!*

Seeing the glass half-full is contagious. Sure, there are hard realities like bills to be paid, money to collect, and negotiations to be generated with your creditors (and maybe your landlord.) Your positive attitude will help shape a positive outcome.

Define the results *you* want. You will always succeed…in producing a result. Don't like the result? Change what was done to produce it! You may have to lengthen or shorten your business hours. You may even have to cut everybody's pay so you all get something.

You may have to sell some inventory at cost, or below your cost, to generate cash. But first, define what it is you want to have happen. Run the numbers. If that is not your strength, get help.

Remember - there are organizations that provide this kind of help for free.

Results energize discipline. For example, make sure that you journal what you did to produce the results, capturing why it looked good along the way (the benchmarks you chose), and what were the first indicators of change in the wrong direction…ones that you may have missed this time around.

The new business owners that I meet, those who are travelling a path to success, have these characteristics in common:

- They ask questions – all the time.

- They take notes to drive their learning – they don't depend on remembering.

- Their eyes "light up" when they talk about their business.

- They are always looking for resources, and;

- They are not afraid to ask for help.

All of the above are indicators of self-starters – people who don't wait for help…they find it. They want to learn and grow. They *love* the process!

If you get discouraged easily; if you find it hard to "get up and get going" in this down economy; if you see life as a series of few successes and many failures (and not as results from which you learn), you probably should not be looking to start a new business.

Find a life coach. Talk to your pastor, priest, or rabbi. Get some help with breaking the pattern of just letting life happen.

Question 9 Assessment

Not yet   *Got it done.*

I am known for my initiative.
1   2   3   4   5   6   7   8   9   10

I am driven to achieve results.
1   2   3   4   5   6   7   8   9   10

I journal about my business.
1   2   3   4   5   6   7   8   9   10

I easily ask for help.
1   2   3   4   5   6   7   8   9   10

I see the glass as "half-full."
1   2   3   4   5   6   7   8   9   10

Add the numbers for your total: _____

45 – 50 = You are on your way!

40 – 46 = You are almost there – just a bit more work to do.

35 – 39 = Good start: know what's next and attack it.

34 or fewer = Are you sure you want to be in business?

Finished Activity Tracking

Started   *Completed*

☐ **I am known for my initiative.**   _____   _____

What I have learned:

_____

_____

_____

_____

_____

_____

☐ **I am driven to achieve results.**   _____   _____

What I have learned:

_____

_____

_____

_____

_____

_____

☐ **I journal about my business.**   _____   _____

What I have learned:

_____

_____

_____

_____

_____

_____

☐ **I easily ask for help.**   _____   _____

What I have learned:

_____

_____

_____

_____

_____

_____

_____

_____

Started   *Completed*

☐ **I see the glass as "half-full."** _____   _____

What I have learned:

_____

_____

_____

_____

_____

_____

☐ _____

_____   _____

What I have learned:

_____

_____

_____

_____

_____

_____

_____

_____

☐ _____

_____   _____

What I have learned:

_____

_____

_____

_____

_____

_____

_____

☐ _____

_____   _____

What I have learned:

_____

_____

_____

_____

_____

_____

_____

Starting Your Own Business?
10 Questions to Consider *Before* Investing a Dime.

Started   *Completed*

☐ _____

_____   _____

What I have learned:

_____

_____

_____

_____

_____

_____

_____

☐ _____

_____   _____

What I have learned:

_____

_____

_____

_____

_____

_____

_____

Question #10
"Do you have a *partner?*"

[NOTE: "Partner" is not used in a legal sense of the word. Presented here is the idea of others supporting your business efforts…everyone from fellow shareholders to members of an Advisory Board.]

Early in my entrepreneurial ventures, it become obvious that several of the aspects of running a business were not skills at which I was especially good.

I needed a partner.

Finding the right partner is often a dangerous journey, as I can testify. I have had many great partners and one extremely bad partner (but…that's another story.)

Research has consistently pointed out that solo entrepreneurs have a less favorable opportunity for business success.

Finding someone (or some *two*) who share your passion for the enterprise, who have similar core beliefs about finances, who have a similar work ethic, who are "other-focused" and not self-focused, and who want, in the end, to reach similar goals – are sometimes hard to find.

In a family owned and run business, I have seen the families split, when fundamental belief systems about truth and how to treat others, although born of the same parenting, diverged and got in the way of business cooperation.

The siblings just never addressed those rivalries in a productive way.

Just as in marriage, opposites seem to attract. So it is in business partnerships – the strengths of the extrovert often compliment the strengths of the introvert (and the opposite is true as well.)

Those wired to seek opportunity and value data will be well served to find a partner who values harmony and seeks the "best" solution.

Complimentary value systems, working together, will achieve far more than working separately.

So, what do you do if you are alone in this new venture?

First, get an *Advisory Board* in place. Find a group of people who offer different business skills, and a range of ages, to help you in the early stages.

You want to find people with whom you can share your concerns, hopes and dreams without fear of repercussions (like you, having an off-the-cuff chat with your banker, who, in answer to his casual question, "So how's it going?" hears what is *really* going on in your heart and head, and the next week, tightens your line of credit!)

Many times, you can find members of your advisory board from the retired businesspeople in the community.

Aim high. Find those who not only have "been there and done that," but also have learned from the process, and are willing to share the wisdom gained from their experience.

Keep in mind, however, that although this group can be an important help in starting your new business, often, the day-to-day work demands that you find someone (or two) who can supplement your strengths, compliment your drive, and support your execution.

Strategic alliances can support you as a "partner."

These kinds of partners may offer solutions for which you have little or no expertise, but are critical in your chain of value.

Sometimes, someone in this group may suggest another business partner who could help.

This can be a blessing, but a word of caution: approach this business relationship much as you would marriage.

Date first. Get engaged. *Then*, get married.

You must first discover how you work together, and learn how to communicate.

Work at transparency on finances, work ethic, morals, value systems (issues such as booking business that you know will fall out the next month just to support the financial story for the banker.)

Hash out these issues.

Make sure that you're "simpatico!"

There is power in partnerships when done well, focused on the same ends, and all working on a purpose greater than each individual!

> **"Though one may be overpowered, two can defend themselves. A cord of three strands is not quickly broken." ~ King Solomon**

Chapter 10 Assessment

Not yet   *Got it done.*

I have an objective view of my strengths and weaknesses.
1   2   3   4   5   6   7   8   9   10

I know how, in my business life, the skills of others supplement me.
1   2   3   4   5   6   7   8   9   10

I have identified supply chain members that might "partner" with my business.
1   2   3   4   5   6   7   8   9   10

I have developed a core of people around me who offer good business advice.
1   2   3   4   5   6   7   8   9   10

I have formally developed an Advisory Board.
1   2   3   4   5   6   7   8   9   10

Add the numbers for your total: _____

45 – 50 = You are on your way!

40 – 46 = You are almost there – just a bit more work to do.

35 – 39 = Good start: know what's next and attack it.

34 or fewer = Are you sure you want to be in business?

Finished Activity Tracking

Started   *Completed*

☐ **I have an objective view of my strengths and weaknesses.**

——————   ——————

What I have learned:

_____

_____

_____

_____

_____

_____

_____

☐ **I know how, in my business life, the skills of others supplement me.**

——————   ——————

What I have learned:

_____

_____

_____

_____

_____

_____

☐ **I have identified supply chain members that might "partner" with my business.**

—————   —————

What I have learned:

_____

_____

_____

_____

_____

_____

☐ **I have developed a core of people around me who offer good business advice.**

—————   —————

What I have learned:

_____

_____

_____

_____

_____

_____

Starting Your Own Business?
10 Questions to Consider *Before* Investing a Dime.

Started   *Completed*

☐ **I have formally developed an Advisory Board.**

_____   _____

What I have learned:

_____

_____

_____

_____

_____

_____

_____

☐ _____

_____   _____

What I have learned:

_____

_____

_____

_____

_____

_____

_____

☐ _____

_____   _____

What I have learned:

_____

_____

_____

_____

_____

_____

☐ _____

_____   _____

What I have learned:

_____

_____

_____

_____

_____

_____

Starting Your Own Business?
10 Questions to Consider *Before* Investing a Dime.

Started *Completed*

☐ _____

_____ _____

What I have learned:

_____
_____
_____
_____
_____
_____
_____

☐ _____

_____ _____

What I have learned:

_____
_____
_____
_____
_____
_____
_____

☐ _____

_____   _____

What I have learned:

_____

_____

_____

_____

_____

_____

_____

☐ _____

_____   _____

What I have learned:

_____

_____

_____

_____

_____

_____

_____

How To Use This
Final Assessment Tool

At the end of each chapter there was a quick assessment for you to determine how you were progressing on each important question raised in that chapter.

The 1 – 10 scale gave you the opportunity to determine where you were in the process, anywhere from **Not Yet** Started to **Got it Done!**

When using the end-of-chapter assessment, if you had never even thought about the issue, a rate of 1 would be valid.

If you had heard about the concept, but never applied it to yourself, or your business, a rating of 2 or 3 would be appropriate.

Don't worry, no one will "grade" these assessments, but the questions do have enormous value in determining if you have considered carefully all the issues important to starting your new business.

Now, we are going to take it to the next level. You will copy the results from each chapter's questions and record them on the following pages. There, you will learn more in-depth about priorities for starting your new business.

Question One Final Assessment

Transfer your results from page 5 and multiply that number by the Weight number, and put the product of that calculation in the Result Column			
	Your Rating	Weight	Result
1. I have penciled it out.		5	
2. I have money set aside.		3	
3. I have access to money.		3	
4. I have set-up a cash flow forecast.		4	
5. I know my start-up costs.		5	
6. I have calculated my break-even point.		4	
Total			

If the Results for Questions **1 or 5** are below 40, the other questions are not important right now.

If you don't know the start-up costs, and have not "penciled out" your business costs and potential revenues, you cannot begin to work on Questions 2, 3, 4, or 6.

As you work on this chapter's questions, you ultimately are looking for a Total Result above 165. Anything less could indicate that there is still much work to do in building the foundation of your new business.

Things I need to do:

☐ _____

☐ _____

☐ _____

Question 2 Final Assessment

Transfer your results from page 17 and multiply that number by the Weight (W) number, and put the product of that calculation in the Result Column			
	Your Rating	**W**	Result
1. I have prepared myself and my family for a change in lifestyle.		5	
2. I'm ready to work long hours.		3	
3. I have the funds to pay my bills without drawing money from the new business.		4	
4. I have written a business plan and my significant other has read it and understands the impact on our current lifestyle.		5	
Total			

If the Results for Questions **1 or 4** are below 40 you have a problem ahead.

You and your family must discuss the sacrifices you are thinking of making, and the change in lifestyle for the benefit of the business. Make certain they are on the same page.

If you are looking to sacrifice your relationships for several years, so that someday you can own a Ferrari (a reward for your change in lifestyle), while your spouse just wants you home for dinner at least three nights a week....you have a major disconnect in lifestyle goals!

These disconnects do not need to be this "radical" either – they can be as simple as your expectation of long hours may be twelve hours a days and your spouse may be thinking ten.

Misaligned expectations become seeds of bitterness.

Your ultimate Total Result for this chapter should be above **140**. Anything less could indicate that there is still much work to do in getting your personal business goals and your family goals harmonized, to deal with your change in lifestyle.

The stress of mismatched expectations robs you of the energy and focus you will need to build your business.

Things I need to do:

☐ _____

☐ _____

☐ _____

☐ _____

☐ _____

Question 3 Final Assessment

Transfer your results from page 27 and multiply that number by the Weight (W) number, and put the product of that calculation in the Result Column			
	Your Rating	**W**	Result
1. I have a general plan for my business future, and I have the support of my spouse or significant other.		**4**	
2. I have talked about my hopes, dreams, and fears, with my family.		**5**	
3. I have talked over the finances with family.		**5**	
4. I have written a business plan, and my significant other has read it, and understands the impact on our relationship.		**3**	
Total			

If the Results for Questions **2 or 3** are below 40, you have a problem ahead – and writing a business plan and showing it to your significant other without these discussions first could cause problems and not generate a positive conversation.

Prepare your family: Discuss your hopes, dreams and fears for your future. Discuss what you have learned to date about finances.

Yes, this conversation is similar to the last chapter: the difference is the focus on making sure there is commitment to supporting the *results* the business produces. Some you will like; some you won't. Your significant other must join you in this up and down business journey.

Your ultimate Total Result for this chapter should be above **140**.

Anything less could indicate that there is still much work to do in getting your support team on board – pulling with you, and all headed in the same direction.

Things I need to do:

☐ _____

☐ _____

☐ _____

☐ _____

☐ _____

Question 4 Final Assessment

Transfer your results from page 39 and multiply that number by the Weight (W) number, and put the product of that calculation in the Result Column			
	Your Rating	**W**	Result
1. I have a written business plan.		**5**	
2. If #1 was an 8, 9, or 10 rating, then assess whether your plan is ready to be reviewed by an objective third party.		**4**	
3. I understand the principles of cash flow.		**5**	
4. I have a cash flow tool (Excel software or the like).		**3**	
5. I have done market research, even at a very rudimentary level.		**4**	
6. I have scoped out the competition, and understand their value proposition		**5**	
7. I have worked on my sales skills.		**3**	
8. I have written my "elevator speech" so that I can effectively talk to potential investors.		**4**	
9. I have a bookkeeper or a bookkeeping system.		**3**	
10. I have worked on my negotiating skills.		**3**	
Total			

If the Results for Questions **1, 3 or 6** are each below 40 (or cumulatively below 120), the other questions are not important right now.

A business plan disciplines the process of identifying the dynamics of the marketplace, and the cash you need to make a viable impression in that market.

A cash flow analysis is fundamental to developing your business plan.

As you work on this chapter's questions, you ultimately are looking for a Total Result above **320**.

Anything less could indicate that there is still much work to do in building the mental framework you need to really begin to enjoy the "business of business."

That enjoyment results from gaining knowledge about business issues you have not deliberately thought about before – and learning that what you thought was a fearful business activity can be understood, monitored and managed.

Things I need to do:

☐ _____

☐ _____

☐ _____

☐ _____

☐ _____

Question 5 Final Assessment

	Your Rating	W	Result
Transfer your results from page 53 and multiply that number by the Weight (W) number, and put the product of that calculation in the Result Column			
1. I have proven that I can make tough decisions.		4	
2. I have thought through what will be different for me working without a team beside me.		5	
3. I have demonstrated in my life that I can think "on the fly."		4	
4. I have proven that I can work without a structured process.		5	
Total			

If the Results for Questions **2 or 4** are each below **40**, the other questions are not important right now.

To help you think through the process of how life will be different, talk to others who have started a similar business; then, reflect on what you have learned and how what you have learned applies to your life circumstances.

As you work on this chapter's questions, you ultimately are looking for a Total Result above **150**.

Anything less could indicate that there is still much reflective work, and journaling, that you need to do, to learn where you have made decisions on the fly, without a manual, and achieved results you didn't like.

I bet, with some reflection, you will find that you can make good decisions even without all the available information.

Things I need to do:

☐ _____

☐ _____

☐ _____

☐ _____

☐ _____

Question 6 Final Assessment

Transfer your results from page 63 and multiply that number by the Weight (W) number, and put the product of that calculation in the Result Column			
	Your Rating	**W**	Result
1. I have developed a strategic plan based on ideas that I have "tested" in the real world.		4	
2. I have developed an implementation time-line, with benchmarks, to keep track of progress.		4	
3. I have a history of idea generation. I have thought about what I have learned from that history that will be applicable to my new business idea.		5	
4. I have collaborated with people who have started businesses similar to mine.		3	
Total			

If the Result for Question **3** is below **40**, the other questions are not important right now.

Not having a history of idea generation will be an impediment that you must manage, but it is not a "show stopper."

Still, it must be managed by the research that you will do with other successful entrepreneurs, determining the steps they found worthwhile…from idea to implementation.

After you have spoken to several successful business people, patterns will emerge that can become steps for you to consider – even a task list – that will help lead you from idea to business implementation.

As you work on this chapter's questions, you ultimately are looking for a Total Result above **136**.

Anything less could indicate that there is still much work to do in developing meaningful lists that will help you develop benchmarks along the path of "getting stuff done."

Things I need to do:

☐ _____

☐ _____

☐ _____

☐ _____

☐ _____

Question 7 Final Assessment

Transfer your results from page 74 and multiply that number by the Weight (W) number, and put the product of that calculation in the Result Column

	Your Rating	W	Result
1. I have demonstrated an ability to communicate well.		5	
2. I have identified the target markets for my product/service.		4	
3. I have identified what motivates customers to buy.		5	
4. I have matched those needs to what I will offer.		3	
5. I have identified what is unique or special about my offering.		4	
6. I can clearly differentiate my offering from the competition.		5	
7. I have developed a list of attributes that make what I'm selling different and compelling.		3	
8. I have developed my pitch.		4	
9. I have said my pitch aloud at least 40 times.		3	
10 I am comfortable, in a casual conversation, telling people what I do and how it will benefit them.		3	
Total			

If the Results for Questions **1, 3 or 6** are each below 40, the other questions are not important right now.

Work on developing your ability to motivate change, inspire confidence and drive action. That ability is enhanced with information – having something useful to communicate about your business.

Understanding what drives your customers to make buying decisions, and knowing how your offering to these customers differs from other providers (competitors), gives you valuable content to communicate.

As you work on this chapter's questions, you ultimately are looking for a Total Result above **320**.

Anything less could indicate that you might want to invest time in the check list at the end of Chapter 7 on page 75.

Things I need to do:

☐ _____

☐ _____

☐ _____

☐ _____

☐ _____

Question 8 Final Assessment

Transfer your results from page 87 and multiply that number times the Weight (W) number and put the product of that calculation in the Result Column			
	Your Rating	**W**	Result
1. I stay as fit as possible to keep my energy up.		4	
2. I understand the product/service category to a high degree.		4	
3. I have developed a positioning strategy.		4	
4. I have developed a personal purpose statement.		5	
5. I have developed a purpose statement for my business.		5	
6. I have a method to remind me that my "passion is a choice."		3	
Total			

If the Results for Questions **4 or 5** are each below 40, the other questions are not important right now.

Purpose drives passion. Get your purpose statements articulated (written) and share those with your significant other or business advisor (see chapter 10).

As you work on this chapter's questions, you are ultimately looking for a Total Result above **208**. Anything less could indicate that there is still much work to do in building the foundation for your passion.

Things I need to do:

☐ _____

☐ _____

☐ _____

☐ _____

☐ _____

Question 9 Final Assessment

Transfer your results from page 99 and multiply that number by the Weight (W) number, and put the product of that calculation in the Result Column			
	Your Rating	**W**	Result
1. I am known for my initiative.		4	
2. I am driven to achieve results.		5	
3. I journal about my business.		4	
4. I easily ask for help.		3	
5. I see the glass as half full.		4	
Total			

If the Result for Question **2** is below **40**, the other questions results are not as important to you as a person who gives energy – instead of requiring energy from others.

Being "driven" does not mean running over others, but it does mean that you are willing to take the initiative at home, at social events, in your spiritual journey, etc. A key to this may, again, be journaling – learning from your own reflections about what is going on in your world.

Optimism is a choice – not just a personality trait. Choose to see the glass as half full. As you work on this chapter's questions, you ultimately are looking for a Total Result above **165**. Anything less could indicate that there is still much work to do in working on being in control of your life instead of letting it control you.

Starting a business takes initiative, but you must develop the discipline to not let circumstances control you – *you* are in control of your response to every circumstance.

Things I need to do:

☐ _____

☐ _____

☐ _____

☐ _____

☐ _____

Question 10 Final Assessment

Transfer your results from page 111 and multiply that number times the Weight (W) number and put the product of that calculation in the Result Column			
	Your Rating	**W**	Result
1. I have an objective view of my strengths and weaknesses.		4	
2. I know how, in my business life, the skills of others supplement me.		4	
3. I have identified supply chain members that might "partner" with my business.		3	
4. I have developed a core of people around me who offer good business advice.		5	
5. I have formally developed an Advisory Board.		4	
Total			

If the Result for Question **4** is below **40**, the other results could well be skewed because you don't have others who validate or hold you accountable for your beliefs about your skills, strengths or weaknesses.

As you work on this chapter's questions, you ultimately are looking for a Total Result above **165**.

Anything less could indicate that you have not taken advantage of the input of others whom you trust to "partner" in advising you about building your business, while still keeping your family intact.

Things I need to do:

☐ _____

☐ _____

☐ _____

☐ _____

☐ _____

Afterword

Congratulations, you have started upon a journey!

The end of one step is just the beginning of another. Life-long learning is like that. The first step, remember, is to understand what the investment must be.

As Jesus reminded those following him one day, "… don't begin until you count the cost. For who would begin construction of a building without first calculating the cost to see if there is enough money to finish it?" Practical advice that is an eternal element of business advice as you begin your journey.

This is an adventure, and just as with those adventures you took in your mind when you were a young child, you never know what is around the bend of your imagination.

So it is in life and in business – around that bend is a result – not success, not failure…a result.

What will you do to produce that result?

What needs to change?

What needs to be strengthened so even bigger outcomes occur?

Do these things, and avoid those behaviors and attitudes that produce a poor result.

As wise King Solomon admonished us, "Know the state of your flocks, and put your heart into caring for your herds (customers – employees.) Whatever you do, do well. For when you go to the grave, there will be no work or planning or knowledge or wisdom."

This book is meant to be a personal process journey. Capture what you observe on the pages provided. Develop plans.

Journal – write stuff down. Learn from your own notes. Find an advisor – someone who will tell you the truth, in love, and encourage you along the path.

And remember, above all else, "Trust in the LORD with all your heart; do not depend on your own understanding. Seek his will in all you do, and he will show you which path to take."

Griff Lindell
Woodburn, OR

Resources

American Association of Franchisees and Dealers
www.aafd.org

American Franchisee Association
www.franchisee.org

BizStats - Free industry statistics and financial ratios
www.bizstats.com

Economic Indicators
www.economicindicators.gov

Elk Mountain Books – Editing & Publishing Consulting
www.elkmountainbooks.com

Entrepreneurs.about.com - Doing a Break-even Analysis
www.tinyurl.com/ygl8yog

Good to Great and other books by Jim Collins
http://www.jimcollins.com

Hoover's - Business Data Resources
www.hoovers.com

IRS – on Starting a Business -
www.irs.gov/businesses/small/article/0,,id=99336,00.html

Kennedy & Olson – Marketing & Advertising
www.kennedy-olson.com

Lindell Associates, LLC
www.lindellassociates.net

Liberty Kidz International, Inc
www.libertykidz.org

Perry P. Perkins - Freelance Writer & Editor
www.perryperkinsbooks.com

SCORE
National - www.score.org/index.html
Portland, OR - www.scorepdx.org

Rachael Weikum Communications
www.weikumcommunications.com

Retail Industry Information
www.retailindustry.about.com/od/organizations

Retail Industry Research Data
www.retailindustry.about.com/cs/reference/index.htm

SBA - Business Startup Help
www.sba.gov/starting_business/startup/basics.html

The Mindt Group - Non-profit experts
www.themindtgroup.com

Motivated Entrepreneur
www.motivatedentrepreneur.com

Perfect Business - Entrepreneurship resource
www.perfectbusiness.com

Toastmasters
www.toastmasters.org

US Government Business Link
www.business.gov

US Patents and Trademarks
www.uspto.gov

Writing Your Business Plan
www.sba.gov/starting_business/planning/writingplan.html

YCHANGE International - Small Business Consultants
www.ychange.com

Index

Quick Order Form

E-mail orders: griff@lindellassociates.net
Order online from www.griffs10.com,
or from your favorite seller.

Postal orders:
Lindell Associates, LLC
PO Box 3172
Wilsonville, OR 97020

Please remit with this form. Check/ money order only.
Please allow 10 business days for delivery.

I understand that I may return this order for a full refund –
for any reason – no questions asked.

___ Starting Your Own Business? @ $14.95ea

Name: _____

Address: _____

City: _____ State: _____

Zip: _____

Shipping:

Please add $2.50 (US) for the first book, and $1.00 (US) for
each additional book.

Quick Order Form

E-mail orders: griff@lindellassociates.net
Order online from www.griffs10.com,
or from your favorite seller.

Postal orders:
Lindell Associates, LLC
PO Box 3172
Wilsonville, OR 97020

Please remit with this form. Check/ money order only.
Please allow 10 business days for delivery.

I understand that I may return this order for a full refund –
for any reason – no questions asked.

___ Starting Your Own Business? @ $14.95ea

Name: _____

Address: _____

City: _____ State: _____

Zip: _____

Shipping:

Please add $2.50 (US) for the first book, and $1.00 (US) for
each additional book.